A Season To Reason: The Irony Of A Loud Silence
By
Ndaba Sibanda
Scarlet Leaf
2020

SCARLET LEAF PUBLISHING HOUSE
TORONTO ONTARIO CANADA
COPYRIGHT BY: NDABA SIBANDA

All rights reserved.

No part of this book can be used or reproduced in any manner whatsoever without written permission, except in the case of brief quotations embodied in critical articles and reviews.

For information address to Scarlet Leaf Publishing House: scarletleafpublishinghouse@gmail.com

Table of Contents

A Season To Reason: The Irony Of A Loud Silence 1
My 'P's 4
Aesthetic And Rhythmic Attributes 6
The Irony Of It 7
Sailing Through 8
My Friend From Overseas 9
Of Course 10
Emma`s Fall 12
Recovery Days 13
The Fates Of Silences 14
Starved Of Love 15
Illusions 16
Slow Guns 17
The Source Of Coffee 18
Compelling Culinary Scene 19
A Journey Of Edifying Urges And Aches 20
Bakithi`s March For Justice 21
Behind Peterson`s Case Was Sentimentality 22
Jungle Doctor And Dweller 23
Good When Stale 24
Cherished 25
Together 26
Careless Counsel 27
What She Said 28
Her Interplay Of Words, Dance And Cadence 29
A Phony Echo 30
The Silence Of Sanity 31
Choked Chalks Flying In The Air 32
A State Of Upheavals 33
Before 34
Elusive Formalities 35
Creating Opportunities 36
True, Blue Or What He Flew 37

The Last Thing On My Mind	38
Hello, I`m Dolly	39
Rendered Redundant	40
A Mirror Of Life	41
Soaked With Blood	42
When She Was Starting	43
The Crowning Of A Queen	44
Shattered	45
Her Obligations and Their Obsessions	46
Tears Of Fears	47
Master Of Ceremonies	48
A Literary Lioness Once Roared And Ruled	50
The Irony Of Life And Love	51
Entrepreneurial Clout	52
Not Boring At All	53
A Force For Change	54
Her Eyes Peeled For Him	55
Prizefights	56
Time And Its Tempo	57
The Perfect Parent	58
Everything	59
Passport Don't Misbehave, What A Close Shave	60
When The Sun Smiled On Fun	61
Money That Languished In Poverty	62
The Value Of Dull Honesty	63
Small Talk	64
Roller Skater	66
Fooling With Her Fluke	68
Food For Thought	69
When Bribes Dance With Betrayals	70
In The Pricky And Tricky Shoes Of The Victims	71
Electricity	72
Imbagwe	73
Hurtful Impostor	74
Lemema Dam	75

Mayhem And Shame In The House 76
Poet 77
The Obscenity Of Conscienceless Beneficiaries 78
Littleness And Sickness 79
The Dance Of Foul 80
No To Xenophobia 81
A Season 83
Monica`s U-Turn 84
She Handled The Situation With Aplomb 85
A Victim Of Malpractices 86
The Intruder`s Story 87
What His Father Told Him 88
What Time Means To Them 89
Of Talent Shows And Shocks 90
Ma`s Maize Meal 91
Dear Headmaster 94
The Rain Money 95
Moonlighting 96
A Victim Of Malpractices 97
The Dynamics of Honor And Influence 98
Why Nomathemba Was Shown The Door 99
The Fate 100
Flowing And Falling 101
Enliven The Stage With That Gospel 102
On Bumping Into Her 103
Echoes Of Discontent 104
A Warm Wholeness 105
Droning Fan 106
Please Tell Me 107
Putrid Purifier 108
Mouth In Cocktail, Eyes On Behinds 109
Flagged By Love 110
The Noisy Stillness Of The Night 111
The Gospel According To Jobstar 112
Eluding Love 113

The Boy`s Unattractive Task	114
In Retrospect	115
The Evening TV News	116
The Floor	117
Tired Tirades	118
Shun or Else...	119
The Man Who Could Hold The Sun Still	120
The Uncontrollable Rhythm	121
Struggling and Snuggling	122
Wise Waters Drank A Young Lady Silly	123
Other Ideas	124
Playing Up	125
The Street Man Rediscovers Himself	126
The Inquisitive Child	127
The Train On A Reverse Mode	128
A Cowardly Act	129
Freedom Chants	130
Crying A Special Cry	131
The Human Experience	132
Bedside Lamp	133
Why Maphala Became Deaf	134
The Shop Mill	135
Lucky Learner Driver	136
The Early Rains	137
If I had A Way...	138
The Elephantine Call	140
Africa's Capital	141
Bring Back Our History And Heritage	142
The Leopard Man's Fate	143
Dance No More	144
One Too Many Losses	145
Malleable Prospect	146
The Outlawed Stalker	147
Tender-hearted Congratulations	148
Why The Mforos Were Ditched	149

The Man's Manifestations	150
Performer And Giver	152
Gogo Mahlangu`s Tears And Tales	154
Of Scary Second-hand Affairs	155
Pauperised	156
The Wrecker`s Heart	157
Blown Away	158
Subzero Fireplace	159
Pre-paid Water Meter	160
Carnages Haunting The Present	161
The Lake Of Vice And Valour	162
The Speaker`s Plea	163
Mopani Worms	164
Beloved Sitshwala	165
The Birthday Dancer Who Stole The Show	166
Tennis Star On The Horizon	167
The Tussle Between Patience And Polite	168
Do You Know Bulawayo?	169
The Past Catching Up With Him	172
A Simple Sweet Snuggle	173
Of Fussing, Fasting And Fastening	174
Their Beautiful Bae	175
Global Social Conscience	176
Stormy Seas And Heartbreaks	177
Dear 2020, What`s My Quote Of The Year?	178
Biography	180

Poetry is nearer to vital truth than history.
                                                            Plato

You truly are wonderful and highly talented.
Submissions Team at Writer's Egg Magazine.

Ndaba, keep on writing the great poetry. –Irene, Editor/Director, Nalubaale Review

My 'P's

My poetry will be power when it advances the right of the poor people to speak without fear

my writing will be right when the rights of the poor people are realised and respected by all

until that day—until that dawn—until that happens my pen will not rest for a second

my pen will be powerless when the need to record the world becomes immaterial

my writing will be obsolete when humanity no longer seeks to gain insight into life

until that day—until that beginning –until that end of ignorance my pen will not rest

my pen will be lifeless the moment it does not say or criticise or mock what has to be said or criticised or mocked

my paper will be poverty

my pen inks out revulsion against prejudice and poverty and persecution

my writing is the writing on the wall of peace and people and progress

my paper does not paper over the cracks of shenanigans and bootlickers

my poetry cannot be flayed or silenced or imprisoned or murdered

my poetry is for the poor—-my poetry is for the people

my writing is for the powerless and the persecuted

it is the medicine for the lily-livered to live again

it is haunting music in the ears of injustices

my writing is for those with ears to hear

its truths are indubitable and invincible

it says the unsayable and thinks the unthinkable

because it cannot be bedfellows with oppression

it is no longer a nightmare waiting to happen

it marks the start of a furious nightmare for those who decide not to see into the soul of the poor

poetry develops children`s verbal and written skills

poetry teaches us the art of creative expression

my poetry will aid one to process experiences and ideas
this poetry will give depression and anxiety sleepless nights
but victims will enjoy and inherit restful and restorative moments
for this poetry is more than a word, it is sympathy, empathy and therapy
for the weary and frustrated , this poetry will seek to soothe them
it will shine a light on the shady and covert fissures of the heart and mind
this poetry is a touch, transition, an observation, reflection and transformation

Aesthetic And Rhythmic Attributes

There are times
 when a simple piece
 transports me into a realm
 estranged from the literal,
 that transition feels supreme,
 that passage feels perfect, spiritual.

. . . .

WHEN I GET LOST
 and lose my mind
 and heart to a scenery,
 by virtue of an imagery,
 a lovely landscape of words
 and sounds and colours and scents—
 please do not look for me in any other
 genre of literature apart from the aroma
 and embrace of an expression and a quality
 of beauty and intensity of emotion—and if you
 find me, please do not expect me to accept anything else
 that lacks the distinctive style and rhythm of my dear genre.

The Irony Of It

Many an unquotable quote was quoted
    The two were unnamed but had names
The two were professed precious doves
They were allegedly devoted albeit distant
For they were always together yet apart
By virtue of that one of them saved money
By going on spending sprees and confessed
To knowing one thing, a huge lack of knowledge
The beginning of the end was ushered in when
One was labelled a compulsive and intrusive liar

Sailing Through

When winds whisper secrets
          into ears of the twittering birds
the fragrance of blooming flowers
dances its way into the nostrils
of lovers and enables them to sail
through thought and distance
and water and time and clouds
into bliss so eternal but short

My Friend From Overseas

He says he wants to visit game sanctuaries and heritage sites
in my country in particular and in Africa in general.
He also wants me to take him to interactive museums
and the rural areas and to the herbalists as well.
I promise to take him on guided game drives to wildlife
conservations where he would see the well-loved
springbok, zebra, cheetah, giraffe and other animals.
He asks me whether he would see lions as well.
I advise him not to worry: plenty of them.
But when he asks me whether it would
be a good idea for him to stroke some of
those animals, I say: at your risk, friend!

Of Course

He travelled until he reached Egodini. It was not Bulawayo`s famous ET Taxi rank. It was the Avoka police station, a place that was infamous for being a torture chamber for the Rhodesian soldiers. The soldiers used to brutalise the communities for various reasons, including being spies or supporters or protectors of the freedom fighters. As Ndlela strode past the gate near a wall of soil his eyes fell on a lonely locked water tap on his right. He counted himself lucky when a young woman in civilian clothes unlocked it and let the water cascade into her oldish plastic bucket. The day was so hot that he was sweating and yearning to quench his thirst for a while. It was not to be because the young lady told him that the tap water on that particular day was too dirty for human consumption. Mouth dry, saddened- he walked along the wall of soil until buildings appeared. The buildings were still Rhodesian in many aspects because their state of paleness and dereliction told one of a story of not having been renovated or painted since the 1970s. There was no single new building except for a new tractor next to a disused structure. That sight brutalised the mind of Ndlela. Was there about as much chance of new buildings or renovations being seen in the near future as donkeys in-flight? On entering what looked like an unloved balcony he saw four officers chatting—of course—in their own language. "Please help me with a letter that enables

me to sell my cattle. "he requested .
"We`ve run out of those serialized forms,"
was the stony response from one of the
officers—-of course—in his language.
How could they say they did not have
such essential stationery? He dragged
himself away from them—angry,
feeling short-changed and helpless.
Such lack and the paleness of
the buildings and the stoniness
of the officers brutalised
his him like a torture zone.
What a "heinous helpless hole".
Of course such was the place
they called Egodini in Avoka.

Emma's Fall

She descended the stairs
    of her lofty ideas about
an exquisite relationship
and that move cost her
reprimands from her friend
for being too unassuming
to attract a serious suitor.
When a small man
whispered a little greeting
she trembled and lost balance
as a storm of emotions speared
through her heart, ratcheting up
a fire whose scent was potent.
When he touched her
it was the masculine scent of
his skin she could not resist—
as she could smell the potency
of love on his breath, and
the future of their chats in his voice.
When she fell he cuddled her—
she fell into his arms, into his
heart, into his care and into
their world, and ascended into
a sumptuous queenship only
thriving on the grace of love.

Recovery Days

The pains chained
    hearts bled and bled
the indignities blinded
bodies yielded to them
the losses laughed loudly
blood heard and heated up
self-esteem came to the rescue
recovery recouped all the glories
and the people`s world was lively
their vision and mission were victories

The Fates Of Silences

At the cost of her liberty, Sethi said it all.
She gave shape to her society`s values.
Sethi articulated her people`s dreams.
At the cost of her everything, she wrote
their consciences. She voiced their fears.
She symbolised the fates of quiet tides.

Starved Of Love

The wife looked at him
    After a beating and queried,
"So this is your rulership?"
The husband opined,
"Don`t question my authority.
I`m in charge, what I say goes".
The wife, hungry with a swollen face
Cried, "Before I lived with you, I didn't know
how painful it is to be ruled. It`s hell on earth.
Oh God, I seek your providence and protection.
I`d rather be loved. I live in bondage. I live in
Perpetual fear. I'm heavy-laden, please help me."

Illusions

After several years of waiting and hoping
　　it became clear to the discerning minds
that the hyped mega-deals purported
to have been clinched had died
a death of illusions

Slow Guns

Not slogans
    She said those slow guns
Drive one into absurdity
"Down with this or that"
When did those slogans
Bring jobs and good life
And peace and development?

The Source Of Coffee

A brilliant and beautiful brew
    You are the real deal, that's true
I didn't know coffee could charm
My taste buds before I came here
Friendly Ethiopian coffee shops
You let me tuck into macchiato
And get lost in its lovely foams
I, Ndaba, become tongue-tied
As its tastiness hypnotizes me
Friendly Ethiopian coffee shops
Possibly your coffee is the best
In the world, or say my taste buds
Friendly Ethiopian coffee shops
You let me nurse your coffee beans
Friendly Ethiopian coffee shops
I marvel at your traditional touch
Ethiopia, what a coffee culture,
My taste buds were not in love
With coffee before I came here
Ethiopia, you are often cited as
As the birthplace of coffee, sure!

Compelling Culinary Scene

Be it traditional cuisine
    With flavor that is genuine—
Be it a French or Asian dish,
One can't ignore the food scene
Now and again crammed
With calming customers
Most cafes in Addis Ababa
Serve a royal assortment
Of dishes, drinks, a squeeze
While great melodies breeze

A Journey Of Edifying Urges And Aches

Her plight was a pitiless poignancy
    A defiant and drunk pregnancy
A time of an unbroken tenderness
Her pleas paled into a furious deafness
Still she learnt that errors are mere lessons
Enriching a series of experiences and passions

Bakithi`s March For Justice

Bakithi set out on it,
　　The activist marched
a brave and noble march;
Bare, bold, blocked; he marched on,
He was the victims` one and only hope
Bhalagwe, was his destination, a crime scene
Bakithi`s sole protest descried human rights abuses

Behind Peterson`s Case Was Sentimentality

The Bulawayo man courted a controversy
    Please beautiful bottom: he pleaded for mercy
The stunned magistrate said: *I crave your pardon*?
Behind her big beautiful behind is me: was his submission
The divorcing man pleaded with the official to grant him
Custody of her backside, saying he would give up any claim
The divorcing wife would have none of it: *to hell with his claims*!
She added that probably the sentimental man had weaning problems!

Jungle Doctor And Dweller

He enfolded the thickness
 Of the forest and its elegance
And whispered into its quaintness
And unearthed the Earth`s silence

Good When Stale

Back in the year 1582
    They tucked into meat
Sometimes it was fresh
Now and then it wasn't
One man whose daughter
Later became a nutritionist
Loved moldy meat and its smell
The daughter flinched at his spell

Cherished

A wallet-friendly bestseller book
became his treasured classic gift
that sailed with him into a world
of adventure and intrigue.
The author`s portraits offered a window
into a variety of cultural experiences,
the reader pictured photographs,
preyed on the author`s paintings,
on the people`s performances,
on the gallery's sculptures.

Together

They met one day
    Yet they did not say
Much but their hot kisses
Were a cocktail of squeezes
That saw them go home together
Before both turned out to be a bother

Careless Counsel

"She's a perfect planter of distrust,
destruction and discord "or so opined
a gossipy wife to a wondering wife-to-be

What She Said

I'm taking myself back, I'm no ball
    Take your tiny ornaments, take all
She wasn't his trash, throwaway trinket
For she had a heart more upright than a ticket

Her Interplay Of Words, Dance And Cadence

Thembi`s taste buds were no stranger
    to seasonings that elevated her thoughts,
the creators of flavors were imaginative,
her voice was a pleasurable, lyrical song,
a short creative ,she spoke on radio at length
of a medium of few words that was her daily diet,
a dish cherished for its amazing tastiness and richness,
for its precision with well-placed spices, her form of food
she dished out , her word choice , a beauty, a saucy delicacy,
she confessed that her favorite dish evoked an intense alertness
to an experience, a precise personal and passionate reaction to an idea,
an event ; preferred for and prepared for its connotations and denotations,
listeners could touch Thembi`s contours, feel her tempo and catch her vocal verses

A Phony Echo

The poor partisan party predictor
    Came up with a mockery of a report
Which dwelled on the performance
Of the party in the general election
The analyst predicated a landslide
But proper predictors weighed in
Their proverb had no kind words
For it was a paralysis of analysis

The Silence Of Sanity

The voices cry out:
    tackle climate change
and the coronavirus
the voters` plea is:
heal the slits and slurs
the bigoted horrors
the big brother sorrows
restore sanity & hope
affordable health
strive for peace
packs and progress
shun polarization
skewed incarceration
for the world hungers
for integrity and dignity
not hegemony
and unitaralism

Choked Chalks Flying In The Air

Teachers threw all their magic marks
    Out of the window and went home
Their starved ears had been patient
Only to become lies` dance-floor
They were the uncarpeted base
In a nightclub of famine and fools
They trooped out , unprepared
And unable to dance to the disco
Of peanuts and pauperisation
Fibs were played as an addition
To the dancing of folly and failings
Their restaurant reserved for none
But hunger, helplessness & hardships

A State Of Upheavals

He kissed pharmaceutical disgraces
    and entrepreneurship races
good riddance
somebody had to explore the parameters
of people's cognitive landscapes
mental health was taking a test
he departed for his ancestral village to farm
and seek psychological equilibrium
the city was laden with stress
fraught with bills, hassles and bustles
the state of the world was a commotion
he sought to find refuge in his village

Before

Sithabile means 'we are happy'
    But Sithabile was in a new state
Of mind, she felt nasty and angry
Pain wasted her at a painful rate
She had plans: grand, ambitious
Before the pandemic happened
Its move insidious and invidious
Its harm a thing never imagined
It affected her and others` conditions
It was political, psychological, existential
She began to think of medical interventions
To huge reinventions: mental and personal
She sought to find comfort in digital media
But there was loneliness and disconnection
Illusions and illusions were its encyclopedia
She needed facts on anxiety and depression

Elusive Formalities

Aged 65, he decidedly declined,
    He knew nothing ritualistic
In all his life ,Ndodana
had not performed a ritualistic
ceremony , that was Ndodana
His wife wished a symbolic
Activity could be performed
On a well-defined occasion
Like having their marriage formalized
Ndodana gave it a rude repudiation

Creating Opportunities

I breathe life into explorations
    Of joy and choice for they say
Either we accept conditions
As they exist or choose a way
Out and create our situations

True, Blue Or What He Flew

L *ike a chick*
    That will grow into a cock
  Qhawe was spotted the day
  He was born. Elders had a way
  Of sniffing at a child`s greatness
  They said he had a rare alertness
  As legend would have it, Qhawe grew
  You`ve no clue, how blue it was but he flew!

The Last Thing On My Mind

There she is, doing a studio album
 with none other than Kenny Rogers.
There she is, one lovely living legend,
an extraordinary singer-songwriter,
teaming up with other musicians.
I`m happy. I see Emmlou Harris.
Do you see them too? The duo?
Linda Ronstadt and our maestro?
Maybe you see Poter Wagoner?
And hear her Number One Hit!
It`s 1974. *I Will Always Love You.*
It`s 1977. *Here You Come Again*
Later: *Two Doors Down.* What a gem.
Heartbreaker. You're the Only One.
9 to 5. But You Know I Love You.
Eagle When She Flies. Fly Dolly!
Let`s go *Dancing with the Moon.*
Better Get to Livin'. Cowgirls Don't Cry.

Hello, I`m Dolly

I could be *Dumb Blonde*. Is there *Something Fishy*? *Daddy Was an Old Time Preacher. Little Sparrow.* I had a series of top ten hits on the country charts. Even *Joshua* knows *Coat of Many Colors. Touch Your Woman. Traveling Man. Jolene. Why'd You Come in Here Lookin' like That. Yellow Roses!* I held the record for the most top ten country albums on the *Billboard Top Country Albums* chart. I`ve the record for the most No. 1 hits by a female country artist. I`m the first artist to have 20 hits on *Billboard's Hot Country Songs* chart in six uninterrupted decades.

Rendered Redundant

He couldn't take it
    anymore, or so he said
so seismic were her lips
that no fly could land on them
the words that shot out of her mouth
were a wild, wild veld fire that left a trail
of devastation and confusion in its wake
the moment she ranted was the instant
he wished there was a mysterious tunnel
he could vanish into like a hunted rabbit
on countless occasions their arguments
sprang from the fact that he was jobless
but he always stated that he was a victim
of an economy that couldn't create jobs

A Mirror Of Life

Her poem appealed to him
    with its pains and passion
he couldn't get enough of it
it was a beautiful throbbing
its ache echoed and echoed
at the lowest part of his heart
it was a beautiful ache, a pinch
his heart pined for over and over
its encores of pains were his pills
her poem pleasured his earlobes
her poem seduced his pained heart
as it weaved together several layers
and aspects of human flaws and foolery
and not only gave him an understanding
of everyday intricacies and enticements
but also a mirror of creativity & authenticity

Soaked With Blood

The world witnessed it in Zim, now it is in Nigeria
When those whose job is to serve and protect
Become law unto themselves, brutality
Becomes their official language
When the innocent protestors
Are barricaded in and shot
With impunity then who
Are the uniformed men
Serving and protecting?
Zimbabwe is weeping
Nigeria is weeping
Africa is weeping
Innocent blood
Is in someone`s
Hands for sure
Africa cannot
Afford to be
Soaked with
Blood
Like
This.

When She Was Starting

Sithethelelo had assumed she was entrenched
 and stable in her pool until it titled & twisted
and shook up her special sweet marital waters,
Pushed to her limits she swam and swam
across a river infested with crocodiles,
and as with several awakenings, all that
had ensued when she was beginning
to dream of thanking her happy hubby
for none other than a job well done!

The Crowning Of A Queen

The sound of your name is music to my ears
　　Yesterday it was sweetie, today it is honey
I wish to call it out every minute for years
Money or not, my day`s yummy and sunny
The sound of your name's my unmatched song
It's an ever-cavorted timeless tune in my heart
I heard it first time and I knew it was lifelong
It steadied on a chart in my heart as my part
More than a melody, it was, a scent of love!
It outsmarted my emotions but I stayed smart
Work cannot disengage us, we're hand in glove
All the storms we weather together, my sweetheart
Your eyes are the moon and the stars that shine above
Just calf love, they said, but I crowned you my future dove

Shattered

Greed, greed
    Your seed, we must weed
Out and thrash in a fiery dish
Greed, greed
Your seed is spite's feed
Unearthed by our shattered earth

Her Obligations and Their Obsessions

Their fixations were intense
 their manifestations brash
she played dump and deaf
the boys drowned and died
in their rivers of crushes
and admirations
ma'am good morning
I wish I could watch you
forever and forever amen
that didn't stop the fresh mentor
from performing her tasks
with an engaging tone

Tears Of Fears

It was five years down
    The road of a stark scam
Haunted by a hangover
The anxieties of the election
Reminded them of a probability
Of a nightmare lurking and looting

Master Of Ceremonies

What a hot happy hostess
    Her hands always keen
To explore ways of caring
She pampered her guests
With warmth and flavours
She had 'specials' on Mondays

Step Back And Reflect
The economist would not sugarcoat it
She told entrepreneurs to be competitive,
To understand the workings of a business
You 're not aggressive and creative enough
To recalibrate and enjoy growth and success

A Literary Lioness Once Roared And Ruled

She roared into cultural glory and pride
    and got culturists and readers ululating.
She dared the culturally dead and deaf.
Against all odds, she penned in Ndebele
and Kalanga. Her books were masterworks,
as each word and each sentence inspired awe.
Considered one of the nation`s greatest writers,
Luba held grammatical and syntactical accuracy
in the highest regard. She established herself
as one of Mthwakazi`s literary intelligentsia.

The Irony Of Life And Love

Irony made a tangible thud
    when Loveless felt in love
with a soul who had vowed
that it was not for her—love!
not on this earth, never, ever
yet she vowed a vow of love,
to love Loveless then and forever

Entrepreneurial Clout

A muscle was flexed
    it loosened and loosened
it was unconcealed, unrestricted,
it was the supremacy of capitalism

Not Boring At All

In a well-attended dinner party
    a friend writer thanked his wife
for sticking with him, a 'boring' guy
but one lady in the crowd begged to differ
no, your man is the most exciting soul alive!

A Force For Change

The little-known organisation
    had to tackle cases of pauperisation
and climate change if it entertained
any idea of becoming a major force
for change in the world, an uneasy one

Her Eyes Peeled For Him

On the lookout
    for any footstep,
any appearance,
she paced about
she kept her eyes
skinned for him
yet he transmuted
into a no-show man

Prizefights

As I read through the volume
    I was dropped into a clear scene
Of frantic family conflicts and politics

Time And Its Tempo

It flowed down the river
    As it did, he felt its rhythm
It was a moment of merriment
It was also a moment of experiment
And he knew that he had to touch it,
Just feel and cup it before it swooshed
And screamed in ecstasy and streamed away

The Perfect Parent

When he was intoxicated
    Irony marked his language
I was the perfect parent
Till I had kids, oh yeah
I committed suicide
Though I didn't die

Everything

On his 34th birthday
    the single parent
was a thrilled heir
of wonderful words
written by his three kids
happy birthday best dad
in the world, our everything

Passport Don't Misbehave, What A Close Shave

12 weird days before the big day`s chorus
I happily hurried into my manager`s office,
in no uncertain terms he politely told me
to come back the next day. When I was free—
precisely 11 days before the big day I said glee,
today is the day to get things really cracking.
Still my superior`s mere glare had me packing
out of his office without uttering a single word!
10 days before the big day I became a word nerd.
9 days before the big day I handed him my request,
8 days before the big day, with delight I hit my chest
for leave was granted. Exactly 7 days before the big day
I danced all day long. Explicitly 6 days before the big day
happened to be a restful Sunday. 5 days before Christmas
happened to be a hectic day. I nearly lost my mental compass
searching for my passport. 4 days prior to Xmas my fugitive pass
was found. 3 days prior to Xmas I was covid-tested. 2 days before
the big day I collected the covid form. Guess what, what did restore
my hopes was a negative lab result! One day before Xmas I travelled
to where my family was. On Xmas day at our joyful reunion we marvelled!

When The Sun Smiled On Fun

I drifted into childhood memories
   I visualised loaves of bread, lorries
of it too. Villagers embraced
it in their way. It paced
into their lives. A holiday.
Christmas Day. What a day.
The beauty of its traditions,
the village ignited into celebrations.
Supersonic radios roared into the night,
the partying pack was my chief delight.
New clothes for kids. Wasn't that special?
New! Forget about 'debt' or 'commercial'.

Money That Languished In Poverty

In his dreams he was one fellow
    who did not to desire to see
stoutness take a toll on his life
but in reality, he was a glutton
his friend had always urged him to be
himself, *for big men are prodigious*—
the one who later badmouthed him,
oh moneyed but poor fiend!, he yelled

The Value Of Dull Honesty

In search of spiciness and excitement
    she, packed, bored, and left someone
who had love, resolve and decency,
a man who strove to be present,
and loved one who hurt her
with his loveless absences
and had nothing to offer
but a series of lies
and lame excuses
her ocean of loneliness and betrayal
cast a light on the worth of company,
nostalgia reflected on her tomorrow,
it took a storm of sorrow
and deception for her
to discover the value
of dull honesty,
happiness
and love
as fate would have it ,
the couple reunited
and revived the fires
of the heart , vowed
never to let boredom
reign and dwarf
beautiful bedroom

Small Talk

Their relationship is too small
or non-existent at all,
They do not know each other at all.
I guess they were not told not to talk
to strangers when they were children!
They are adults and the ice has to be broken.
Adults are expected to say at least a few words
at the bus stop, in the doctor's waiting room,
at the train station or in the banking wall.
When did you last visit a smart shop assistant
or a smiling hairdresser or a waitress
and you were not called a 'friend'?
Let us face it—small talk allows us to exchange ideas
and information in order to determine shared interests,
It has given birth to numerous marriages and deals!
In our business aspect of life we need good—
yes good conversational skills to make milestone deals,
Be it social or personal aspect of life, we need to chat a bit.

• • • •

SMALL TALK IS LIKE getting into unfamiliar terrain—
You don't want to see a person's face blush or frown
or lips pout or to make someone quite uncomfortable!
One middle-aged man caught sight of a young lady
and decided to get her to open up by remarking," You
look stunning like my ex-wife! Where are you from?"
There is an air of unfamiliarity and safety
about small talk that makes cool guys like
Weather and Current Affairs fall victim.
Poor guy- Sports- he is not spared either,
These guys are roped in and crowned sacrificial lambs,
Current Affairs once told me there is nothing current about this!

Weather says this way of striking up a conversation is not cool,
Sports warns that if this game continues, he won`t play ball!
Current Affairs believes this strategy is archaic-FULLSTOP.
One chap dragged Mr. Weather into victimhood
by saying, "Today`s sunny. The sun looks beautiful and big!"
Had the friendly chap in a suit run out of something to say?

• • • •

MAYBE THERE WAS A SOLAR eclipse blurring his sight!
    Like the beauty of the African sun before sunset,
    Small talk galvanised both of them to take photos.

• • • •

SMALL TALK IS A GREAT tool for beginning a relationship
    It is a willingness to talk to someone else.
    An effort to sustain a conversation.
    Small talk is not that small because it breaks the ice
    and beams the smile of humanity.
    It builds amity and unity.

Roller Skater

Night sleeps
    a rider rolls
ohs and wows
caresses and cries
done deal
off home
up the lump
down the road
a smell of lies
a bag of tricks
all he has
all there is
the road winds
the road dances
dust puffs
wheels blare

. . . .

EASES DOWN
    steadies his voice
    he arrives
    sweaty arms
    not really sure
    a long breath
    lies he shoots
    lies she eats
    lipstick sheens
    its shade betrays
    feminine scent
    seals the deal!
    what the heck?
    you were up to...?

it`s war time
it sucks big time

Fooling With Her Fluke

How many times does fortune knock on the door?
    she looked back and counted her blessings
awed by the trajectory of her life
it was a serendipitous leap that
saw her assume the position
of executive officer
after the resignation
of the incumbent
she never wanted
to sleep on the job
but somehow
she did

Food For Thought

To swig because
        something is given
is to tempt and test
the patience of such
comrades as Sir Vomit
or Constipation too far
like a silly bare tongue
kissing Ms. Electricity

. . . .

TO DANCE TO THE TUNE
of a sick fire is only musical
when the extinguishers
and firemen are working
to make a series of turnarounds
till one is really dizzy and does
not know where and how to stop
is to have an upside-down dream
whose closest relative is Nightmare

When Bribes Dance With Betrayals

The neighbor told him a story
    of a man of incredible strength,
one who followed proscriptions,
one who wouldn't drink alcohol.
After a deal of trial and error
his lover discovered the source
of his strength, his *hair*. Well!
She betrayed him and divulged
the secret to his eager enemies.
Once the man`s hair was cut,
the strength he had was history,
hence he was blinded and enslaved.
"If a man of strength, a famous judge,
can lose his strength like that, well, who
are you to think you can win these battles?
"Good luck. And pray". The neighbor said.

In The Pricky And Tricky Shoes Of The Victims

His name was Trust
    Though no one trusted him
A club of thugs was doing bloodcurdling acts
Usurping the innocent people`s cattle and land
Beating up hardworking owners and herders of the cattle
There was bloodshed and all the prints of mad destruction
One day vociferous and violent Trust fell out of favour with the club leaders
The thug was hounded and horrified as the club swooped on his cattle and land

Electricity

Unite and look for Electricity
   Victims and all—please search for him
That side of town is dark and dangerous
Because of thugs and their anarchic ways
Let there be light in that neighbourhood
Not evil vandalism of freedom and people

Imbagwe

This was a bread basket, a jewel;
    This is now a wreck of boiling Anger,
Always hovering about like an unusable imp
is none other than Hunger.
How many African leaders ever condemned
the man-made free-fall into economic turbulences?
Who condones this degeneration into a basket case?
What do they have to show for years of independence?

Hurtful Impostor

He resorted to brutality at the slightest of provocation...
    Therebhulu held back his disdain. Or so they thought he had.
Then Therebhulu unleashed terror in Zhombe—
resulting in decimated populations.
Therebhulu proved to be a false advocate
of peace and harmony and progress.
He was a fake preacher of love.
He abused women and slaughtered many
unsuspecting neighbours at night with his
hardhearted trained dogs.
Lying and viciousness were part of his DNA.
Depravity and damage were his pastime—
He was kicked out of his paternal village.

Lemema Dam

Please don't slip away
    From the people's love and care,
Dam of posterity and forefathers,
Dam of peace, love and livelihood,
Here they come—and steal and rape you,
By stabbing your delicate bowls with their vice,
As if the anus is a playground for messing up with,
Now the pains you go through surge into the communities,
They cry the orphans' ignored cries as they bleed dams of anguish,
But soon those pains will turn into rivers and oceans of resistance,
The love you have they turn into their favourite playground of hatred,
The livelihood into their damaging game of greed and dominion and distress.

Mayhem And Shame In The House

There is hullabaloo
    in this house of order
Moved is no motion,
but seen is utter commotion
There is drama so sour
walking naked from this house
There is elbowing and yelling
in this august house of edicts
There seems to be lawlessness
in the house of laws and dignity
Can orderliness and laws
come from a din of lawlessness?
Please don`t give them the floor
to see and sneer at us again
Tomorrow they will say
we`re our worst enemies
You say this is not about the 'worst'
Yes, this is about our future and pride!
Can they hold back their giggles
if shame walks naked in our house?

Poet

P*lease* proud poet perfect your craft
　　　Organise thoughts into lovely words
　Edit to capture an image or a feeling
　Trim the piece into a compelling pearl

The Obscenity Of Conscienceless Beneficiaries

A disgusting situation. Companies are perishing.
Corruption is flourishing. The economy is ailing.
The heirs are rejoicing. The poor are languishing.
Haemorrgaged by corruption. Obscene salaries
are blind to the social and economic hardships
the ordinary citizens are going through.
They can dance on the floor of poverty knowing
very well that they are being supported
by those who have the might to halt it.
Is this nation going somewhere or nowhere?
Protection of looters is an indictment of integrity.
Political affliction is the criteria for righteousness.
If you want local companies to perish, belong to them.
Everything is politicized. Jobs and development projects.
Kickbacks come first. The people come last. Graft is their idol.
Ailing government enterprises have been gobbling up millions
of dollars in hefty salaries and allowances at the expense
of service delivery and lowly-paid employees.
Do they act in the national interest?
Is this what they call a zero tolerance approach to corruption?
Will they take decisive measures to eradicate corruption in all its forms?

Littleness And Sickness

There was an eruption
    of toxic corruption
It spread across the nation—-
suffocating cities and companies
Wreaking havoc with ethics
and professional practices
Rhetoric grew louder and louder—-
There was little effort to curb the scourge
Enterprises which were distressed and sucked dry—
sadly succumbed to the deadly disease
The nation was gripped by a liquidity syndrome—-
Frustration and hopelessness drove decent citizens out

The Dance Of Foul

The auditorium was a bustling with expectant and wounded victims and peace-makers,

The slim but calm magistrate of time and season was speaking in her personal capacity:

'The fouling and hounding of the innocent peace-lovers and peace-makers will not in any way exonerate the hooligans and their cohorts from dancing to the tune of their musical compositions'.

No To Xenophobia

The sanctity of life must be respected.
At all costs, humanity supersedes other considerations.
Brothers and sisters, abstain from hatred and xenophobic attacks,
Think of the possibility that you could be attacking a blood sister or brother.
The illustrious ideals and sacrifices of the departed champions for African emancipation
must be respected and upheld. The pestilence of violence is a slap in the face of Pan-Africanism.
On the other hand, the scarcity of jobs and other socio-economic opportunities is a plague,
Economic liberation of all is a process that must be prioritised by all African nations.
Economic liberation does not share a bed or a chair with wanton economic plunder,
It has absolutely nothing to do with cronyism and fiefdom and kickbacks.
No to bad leadership because it gives birth to many social ills
including abject poverty and unfettered corruption and illiteracy.
No to abuse of Africa's resources because such misuse drags
away this continent from meaningful development and prosperity.
African leaders shouldn't bury their heads in the sand and merely
condemn the spates of violence from the comfort of their offices.
There has to be a holistic and concrete approach to the scourge.
Now is the time for African leaders to accept complicity and act responsibly.
It is not enough to call for the cessation of that brutality without addressing
the economic and political brutalities at home which force their people to flock to South Africa.
No to the destructive demon of xenophobia for there is no foreignness
between brothers and sisters joined together by history and heritage.
For dear Africa to conquer some of her challenges and indeed prosper

sound economic policies must be shored up by political willingness and discipline

A Season

• • • •

Feast.
Festive mood.
There was a joy of joys.
A talk of talks smartly coupled with a walk
of walks. The grandparent of celebrations. For the majority
of the citizens it was the cheeriest and greatest season of the year
out there. It was a time to soak in the fun. To wine and dine. A time to bask in
the sun and share the spirit of cheerful mirth with family and friends. However, there
was a call for people to spare a moment for the less fortunate. It was also a season to reason.
As the celebrants lost themselves in a festive mood, in the fun of the season in the jive
and dive of it all, they were humbly encouraged to consider the plight
of other human beings in the cold or along smelly alleys. There was a prayer
and a plea for spreading the spirit of good will and love and joy to the
hungry and destitute. At the end, there was a river of
drunkenness , debauchery , malice and commersialisation
souls drowned in. There was a grimly side on the
roads. Confusion and carnage.
Was that the true spirit
of the season?
I
rest my case.

Monica`s U-Turn

Monica had resolved to ignore
everything to do with the holiday
she wanted to sleep and snore
outside fun was having its WAY
the holiday season was upon them
fun and gaiety ruled really supreme
revelers felt a joyous jumping abandon
for how long could she resist that fun?
sleep told her to give it a little break
it warned-if not-her night was bleak
this galvanised her to join in the season
a nun- she went wild and said it was fun!

She Handled The Situation With Aplomb

An amazing presence on the site
    Armed like a dangerous dissident
Equipped with her knowledge
With neither a gun nor a bomb
She carried the following tools:
Splunk and snort and tanium
She had an ArcSight too
Not an AK 47 but an ELK!
She got some men really wilting
When her ethical hacking paper
Dropped on their laps by mistake
What a stop-nonsense certificate!
She explored the besieged site
As an experienced threat analyst
A malware or a forensic specialist
A smart incident handler or manager

A Victim Of Malpractices

It seems to be collapsing
    like a pack of crazy cards
today price hikes, shortages—-
queues, loading shedding and all
does this long- raped economy
have to swallow all the trash ever?
small wonder it seems to be
failing to economize on bills—-
with travelling bills bullying
health, hospitals are victimized
if this economy is cared for
why it is a comatose corpse?
the corrupt live and thrive
the poor can`t even survive
as they hop from scarcities
to duplicities and uncivilities
this economy is not an enemy
but a victim of inefficiencies
it has unlivable structures
that give refuge to miseries
its fares fool and fail travelers
its banks can't be banked on
its hospitals are no longer
hospitable but horrible
its cash cashes on victims
of cartels and corruption
the price of fuel is fuelling pain
with no gain for the paying poor

The Intruder`s Story

The man came home during the lunch hour only
    to see a man in overalls relaxing in their room.
Was she feigning sleepiness? There was an intruder
in the room, and she was snoring like a tractor.
"I was just driving in a nail here and there. And
tightening that small screw in the door".
Or so explained the huge intruder after being
asked what exactly he was busy with.
The snoring wife`s husband couldn't
believe what he was hearing...
Was he feigning drunkenness?
His T-shirt had words: *fake it*

What His Father Told Him

Son, grow up and know that impudence
and insolence have not been wiped out
of this world we love and live in.
Son, your former friend might have said
those insolent and impudent words
but listen, you have your life to live.
Having one's ego wounded is something
bitter to endure, but ask yourself: will
revenge add value to your life?
Ego and brazen boldness have casualties—
your anger could be at boiling point
but think about the consequences.
Son, brush aside that bitterness of spirit,
kick out that rancour like someone
spewing off gall, and heal yourself.
For rancour is like a gall problem—
it will hold you hostage and keep you
away from healing and happiness.

What Time Means To Them

Telling the tots that time
    Does not always mean play
Can be a story that gets into
The left ear and leave through
Their right one as they go out
To play and hang out with other
Eager toddlers or preschoolers

Of Talent Shows And Shocks

A *little something*
     For the listeners
Was a song sung
By a youthful fellow
On OMG Mars
Has Got Talent Show
If the fast-paced lyrics
Were meaningful
His breathless singing
Surely didn't show it
Ears were starved
Of something delightful
He didn't seem mindful
Of his pace and tone too
I guess ears on Mars felt
Shocked and short-changed!

Ma`s Maize Meal

She brought in
    with her a silver pot
into which she discharged
water before assigning the vessel
to sit silently on the warming plate
When the silver pot was steaming
the water inside it was screaming
emotive gurgles that got her
toting guarded quantities
of *mealie-meal* and stirring
She left the porridge to simmer
and thicken for some time—
the aroma emanating
from the bubbling
was mouth-watering

The Best

Ntabeni`s *cabinet appointment* party was graced
by the president, a man who danced like a hyperactive kid.
The attendees didn't know whether the dishes and drinks
the president had tucked into were the root of his vivacity.
Before the elite guests` departure and dispersal Minister Ntabeni
stood up and thanked the president for his exemplary leadership.

Like most unctuous political appointees, the minister in the president`s office

described the president as the best gourmet , dancer and leader in the world!

A Beginning Of Bravado
Chapped lips seemed wasting away
A victim to a dry or windy weather
Sores in the corners of her mouth
Her eyes had a distant and tired look
When she was young and fresh and funny
Boys puffed smoke at her as if to impress her
But in the end they impregnated her with odium
For she knew cigarettes were forbidden to them
Thirty- four years down the road love dawned on her
She looked hungry and fresh for its ambers and angles

Dear Headmaster

It is with a great sense of utter distress,
disillusionment and horror that I write
this little wake-up letter.
There is abject poverty of teaching and learning
at your school, no wonder learners are leaving that
institution in a huff and in great numbers.
I have heard your teachers say you are a principled
man with the welfare of our children at heart
and a mind of encyclopedic proportions.
I beg to differ. You are the most shameless, useless,
destructive and stubborn headmaster to lead
that once-great centre of excellence.
Your bootlicking teachers shower praises upon
you because you allow them to doze off or visit the
beerhall or friends during school hours!
Your argument that independent journalists are
taking a dig at you because of your political affiliation
with that old party is clearly hollow and untenable.
Dear headmaster, you lost the essential moral compass
befitting of a true leader and father long ago. Anarchy stalks
the school yard. Don`t deny that you have lost our trust!
Before each Annual General Meeting your mouth conceives a baby
called Lies. Come the AGM your pregnant mouth shamelessly gives birth
to Lies! Know what-I am taking my children out of that School of Lies!
Your office roof has carved in. You cannot pretend to be blind because soon
the debris will fall upon you and bury you in your heap of denials. The school
is in a pathetic state. Do yourself a favour, pack up and vacate!

The Rain Money

They say what?
    They say the looters
Have upped their game
How could they loot
The money for the rains?
Now the land is dry and dying
If you thought this were
A laughing matter—think of
The dying cattle and maize plants
Think of the unbearable heat
And the possibility of people starving
To death because of such 'looting'

Moonlighting

Continental Massacre
   was his 'stage' name
some said he was a joke
massacring his new name
by being a clear claimant
but he said he was not
he said he was a writer
and a wonderful musician
yet he neither sang a song
nor wrote a poem or a story
people asked what was under
his belt as a writer or a musician
but he never stopped claiming
to be moonlighting, not daydreaming!

A Victim Of Malpractices

It seems to be collapsing
    like a pack of crazy cards
today price hikes, shortages—-
queues, loading shedding and all
does this long- raped economy
have to swallow all the trash ever?
small wonder it seems to be
failing to economize on bills—-
with travelling bills bullying
health, hospitals are victimized
if this economy is cared for
why it is a comatose corpse?
the corrupt live and thrive
the poor can`t even survive
as they hop from scarcities
to duplicities and uncivilities
this economy is not an enemy
but a victim of inefficiencies
it has unlivable structures
that give refuge to miseries
its fares fool and fail travelers
its banks can't be banked on
its hospitals are no longer
hospitable but horrible
its cash cashes on victims
of cartels and corruption
the price of fuel is fuelling pain
with no gain for the paying poor

The Dynamics of Honor And Influence

A court subpoena demands that we
hand over a record of every letter
and email or little note we have.
The people we're dealing with are a bunch
of greedy politicians and business moguls
with unlimited resources, pride and power.
They take pride in flexing their financial muscles—
for them, power and status are the brushes to
paint themselves with righteousness and integrity.

• • • •

IF EVER THEY GET THEIR dirty hands on our correspondence
and all our private information, alas, there's no telling
what they'll use that evidence, that information for.
More than half of the world is
coerced to walk along a rude road
of skewedness and awkwardness.
Why are the scales of righteousness
and fair-mindedness easily tipped
in favour of the affluent and potent?
Where are the values of those who
hold positions of power and authority
when equal access to justice for all is zero?
Isn't justice a privilege for the powerful
and the wealthy? Why is the protection
of the law out of reach for the majority?

Why Nomathemba Was Shown The Door

She used to have a big bag of tricks and excuses
    like: I had a medical appointment and what nonsense
but behavioural and academic expectations
were a hymn that each student was drilled in
dress code: wear a normal school uniform
and a track suit for extra-mural activities only
hairstyle: no fashion statements or fancy hairstyles
hair may not be bleached or dyed or cut in extreme style
absenteeism: no student may miss a lesson without a valid reason
unless instructed—no sitting or loitering along the corridor
jewellery: a wrist watch may be worn, but no other
no to tongue or nose piercing or visible tattoos
under no circumstances will make-up be permitted
the same for extremely long nails or colorful lipstick
no bad language or bullying or carrying of weapons
smoking and drinking of alcohol will lead to instant expulsion
of course laws are there to be broken—so said Nomathemba
as she came to school dead drunk with *mbanje* and *nyaope*
her artificially long nails could stab a dead lion into life
and her lipstick and dyed hair could pass for some bloodbath
and then she engaged in the bullying of girls and under-the-desk
baby-sitting of boys until the school authorities kicked her out

nyaope or *whoonga* or *wunga*—-a highly addictive street drug widely available in South Africa

mbanje, SiNdebele for marijuana

The Fate

Ever wondered
    About the destiny
Of Africa?
Of the world?
Is the destiny
Of the world
In the hands
Of the leaders?
Of the citizens?
Of the youth?
Demanding issues:
climate change
racial justice
gender issues
misrule
corruption
greed
hegemony

Flowing And Falling

Her fine voice flew—-
    Cascaded into his ears
His heart, his very soul
She was far, though through it
She bickered, beat gently, gently
Like the rains from the heavens
Her voice was the noise he pined for
It pattered a repetitive, real presence
Plashing and patting him on the pulse
Leaving him to drown in waters whose saltiness
Seemed to fight fierce battles against the sweetness
And soreness of missed targets and tantalised emotions

Enliven The Stage With That Gospel

Expose their eyes and ears to the pedagogy
    of fresh speech and movement and choice
blow away their silly sirens of ruins
administer baptism to their brains
bolster support for justice
for they neither see
nor hear

On Bumping Into Her

She told me about it. The story of guests
who rent cars or a bunch of bunk beds.
I didn't know what a backpacker hotel
was. She told me she was a backpacker.
No wonder she had her little supplies,
her personal belongings. Her things.
At one time I know she stuttered:
I didn't catch some words she uttered.
Did she belong to who? I didn't get it?
Did she talk of her things or her thighs?
Then there was a lesson on travelling,
travelling on budgeted accommodation.
On a backpack being smaller
than a rucksack, on getting a pack.
I said ok: sackpack , backsack,
or knapsack or whatever. Bye!

Echoes Of Discontent

They sing a defiant painful song
    they echo the same sentiments
bulldozers and graders won't ever
uproot them from their resolve
they say they would rather be called
job-grabbing foreigners and refugees
than go back to their motherland
a hotbed of corruption and decay
they say they are running away from
known hopelessness and senselessness

A Warm Wholeness

I found out—
    pouring out
 her heart into me
 that she was my glee
 I felt its pounding presence
 magically turning love`s absence
 into a delightful deluge of affection
 I felt a completeness, a prized passion

Droning Fan

From a distance comfort looked
    like the axis of the life there
his nakedness spread across
his bed like some tentacles
he lay on an immense bed
that struggled to breathe
and radiate its own kingly
comfort and accouterments
the room was just blistering
white sheets and multi-coloured
bedspreads beautified the sight
central conditioning seemed
to have drowned in slumber
at that time and particular night
the droning fan sought to blow
air in his nudity`s direction but
it succeeded to keep sleep away
the whir of the fan drove his mind
into itchy and jerky pensiveness

Please Tell Me

Read me a book about talking animals and birds
and I will show you a group of people chirping
tell me about the love of money and I will tell
you about the worshiping of material things
tell me about a man who was relaxing in his chair
and fell off and I will tell you of witch-hunters
tell me about writers who have outstripped
their readers, and I will tell you the poets` story.
tell me about wrecked nations and I will tell you
about a country that will emerge from the ashes

Putrid Purifier

All the poison and perfume
    you seek to swallow and inhale in
as you loll out your long tongue to wipe
off the mess and madness of the perpetrators—
is a source of concern and a matter of pure perfidy

Mouth In Cocktail, Eyes On Behinds

What an impressive swine—
 he was downing glasses
of red -tinted wine
eyes on big rears.

Flagged By Love

Her voice stung by bitterness,
    she roared over the phone,
offside was a lioness,
but it was done.
Her voice rose, trailed;
the dreaded flag was up,
her heart bled ,wailed;
but it was bitter to sup.

The Noisy Stillness Of The Night

The nocturnal visitors were slotting
a little cold stillness into
her yawning mouth
when her husband
stormed in.
She woke up, only to hear the
pattering of the rain outside,
and feel the coldness of her cat—
which had secretly snuggled
under her blankets.
The black and white fat cat
mewed a little as if saying:
I don`t think it`s cool
to chew things noisily
in one`s sleep!

The Gospel According To Jobstar

I heard that several people seek
    to secure gainful employment
the atmosphere is competitive
as the jobs seem to be elusive
I heard that companies that seek
to employ people are as varied as
the types of workers they search for
all they want are those who stand out
she said grades alone are not enough
I thought intelligence was all and end all
she claimed personality was a big factor
social engagement an added advantage

Eluding Love

Two biological sisters
    stuck in a bitter feud
fought like they were
heartless and headless
impishness itself
neighbours sent
snakes on errands
of loathing instead
of loving as if both
we were profiting
one neighbour wondered
why some people carried
heavy loads of jealousy
and heartlessness when
life was lived just once

The Boy`s Unattractive Task

A boy was sent to fetch money from a certain house owner,
at the gate the boy saw an old man seated on a wooden stool.
He just shot passed him as if he were a log without a mouth,
He had no business with a mere stranger –he told himself.
Upon finding no one else in the yard, he went to the old man—
faced with the unenviable task of being human and humble.

In Retrospect

Bhoyibhoyi was young and full of energy.
    He had misled many a pretty girl—
Pregnancies, abortions and lies
haunted him but as he looked
back it dawned on him that
he had to look forward.

The Evening TV News

She never missed the main evening news,
it was as if she were addicted to it;
but then that hour had its drama.
Her children wondered why she watched it
because almost during every news hour
she would curse and flinch.
Words like "Look at these bastards now?
Oh please give us a break. Shit again!"-
always escaped from her mouth.

The Floor

Feels stiff, sick
    stings buttocks
like it has flair
all night long
it fools sleep
hollowness
it sighs too

Tired Tirades

A sick slowness to a crisis,
    A foolish fastness to non-issues.
Is this about diverting attention?
Is this about bankruptcy of ideas?

Shun or Else...

A few years ago I stumbled upon a street preacher
in Sunnyside, Pretoria, encouraging the unmarried
who cared to listen to him to shun masturbation
because it is immoral. I paused and pondered.
In Yeoville, Johannesburg, I recently bumped
into a passionate street evangelist who paced
across the busy pavement, saying people
should shun spiritual wives and husbands.

The Man Who Could Hold The Sun Still

The playful women whispered
    about the tenderness of Time,
his boss bemoaned the man`s
slowness and carefreeness,
but somehow , somewhere
that trait made him topical.
He was like that—a man
who executed activities with
the unhurried steadiness of
someone who could halt his
watch or whose day had more
than mere twenty-four hours.
His emblem of the slowness of
a snail was evident everywhere-
the pace at which he ate food
or dealt with a crisis or an event—
the manner he walked or talked
or upheld his conjugal rights.

The Uncontrollable Rhythm

Inside his heart there is heat,
    Inside his body there is a beat.
He hears a voice of deafness.
Marvels at its unstill stillness.
There is a pace he has to party to,
Its throb is poetic, its pacifying too.

Struggling and Snuggling

A fierce battle of emotions,
    a drama of elbowing and dragging.
Privacy won the physical and emotional scuffle
as she found herself nestled on the summit of regrets.

Wise Waters Drank A Young Lady Silly

Some drama happened at a place called Hontana.
　　It was a one-woman show, and she was not by
any chance a stand- up comedian of sorts.
On the concrete pavement she decided
to swing her body such that her legs
flew in the air, whilst passers-by
feasted on her palpable frolics.
Chaps who "saved" her from
her fall from grace said pint
had smashed her silly.

Other Ideas

An overseas business trip well thought-out
    every detail done with meticulousness
no foot put in the wrong place
no wrong word uttered
the elders say food scatters off the plate
when the mouths are agape and ready
an overseas business trip tripped
by indistinguishable players
Unforeseen and fuzzy players seeking to void
and mock noble efforts of putting food
on the table and the schooling of kids
these players are shameless
faith is a weapon that is unbreakable
it has other ideas and windows
that are powered by light
and a winning character
the blurry forces have been castrated and voided
they have melted away into noisy nothingness
the chains of confusion have been broken
progress has been anointed

Playing Up

If you asked me
    I would not hesitate
to say that the Internet
on my cell phone today
is playing a mindless game
with my set and serious mind.
Imagine it says I have a working
network connection when I cannot
access my emails and what-have-you.
It reminds me of a man who said he loved
his lover but his actions screamed words like:
I am not in your life and we have no connection!

The Street Man Rediscovers Himself

He used to be blind to his self-damage
it had not dawned on him that he was lost
but suddenly his directionlessness reeked
summer switched off rather too quickly for the vagrant
his body was used to all kinds of weather and seasons
but suddenly he found himself struggling with the changes
he had never thought of being examined by a doctor before
he had never been in a decent room for some fifteen years
but suddenly he wished he had a doctor and a decent room
his feet were used to drifting towards many refuse bins
he rummaged through them—his mouth dirty with dirtiness
but suddenly he felt the unhealthiness of the forays and foods
his home consisted of streets and roads and shacks and passages
his clothes consisted of tattered and nondescript cloths and dirtiness
but suddenly he felt a longing to be in a house and tucked in proper clothes
his music consisted of obscenities and yelling and drunken snoring and singing
his relatives were vagabonds and strangers and drug-abusers and stray pets
but suddenly he pined for the music of the soul and closeness of humanity
as he set out on his journey of soul-searching hopelessness`s odour rioted
as he embarked on his mental trip of introspection he felt he owed himself a life
but he had to deal with his limitlessness of wandering and move into purposefulness
he wondered in his mess where the hand of mercy and change could be accessed
he became aware of his mess and the mercilessness of his decisions and actions
there was no doubt in his mind that he had to recover and rebrand and restore

The Inquisitive Child

She was barely three years old
when she asked her dad
whether he was content about
going to work and coming back
every day and paying many bills
month in month out without fail.
One day she asked her mom,
"please tell me the meaning
of this: when I`m hungry or
thirsty I eat food or drink water,
go to the loo and empty ,and then
go hungry again, and begin the cycle?"
She wondered about the sequences
of many activities, like sleeping and
waking up, buying a housing and
spending the better part of one`s life
away from it, especially "living" at
work or spending time with total strangers.
The answers she got from her parents,
in her opinion bordered on puerility
and insincerity because she felt that life
had to be more abundant and meaningful
that a series of activities –even a so-called
expert on happy living did not impress her.

The Train On A Reverse Mode

MaZondo bowed down and buried her head
between her legs. She felt dizzy and tired.
The queue at the busy border post
was long and ostensibly frozen.
She had been in the business of
selling her wares for years.
Her train of thoughts
took her to her youth.
The independence
train was backing .

A Cowardly Act

Tension pulsed.
　　Sweat poured out
of her pores.
A thief welded
a knife aloft.
It glared at her
as if the blade
longed to sink
into her skin.
Its sharpness
glowed as the
robber looked
set to plunge
it into her chest.
She beseeched
and prayed
and pleaded
and shivered.
It was menacing
and dropping
when she woke
up with a squawk!

Freedom Chants

It was her philosophy to forget herself, her environment and let her body sing songs of freedom in that small room. She let loose everything, and her body vibrated with the innocence of relief as she responded to the duty of nature.

Crying A Special Cry

I couldn't have asked for more. I was learning to learn
my learners` learning styles when he was student.
Then a few years down the line he wrote me a message
so unforgettable that I pinched my body for sobriety.
'I`II never forget you in my life. I couldn't speak
and write in English with the fluency I`ve now."
I felt like breaking down from crying
from happiness and humility.

The Human Experience

As the student of life waited for her results—
  after having done everything to her best ability
unsettling uncertainties visited her mind
she was certain that the results could either
be positive or negative because of
the unevenness of the human landscape

Bedside Lamp

Where is your light?
        Please shed light
on why it is dim.

Why Maphala Became Deaf

Maphala lost his pension to their bungling,
    thirty-eight years of sweat gone into evaporation,
He had a funeral cover but the meltdown
swept away everything and left him uncovered.
Here and there he had invested but a political parasite
of ineptitude made him look like an unfocused breadwinner.
He could not swim in mess; he was languishing in the jumble—
everything was stuck in the endless middle of the imposed muddle.
Years later when the masters of ineptitude swam in mess
but continued to preach development, Maphala became deaf.

The Shop Mill

She looked for a hole to dissolve into and become history.
    However, on and on dispersed their story.
The story of her and a delivery man who was caught
delivering his boxes of masculinity to her.
The rumour mill was unstoppable
on the premises and beyond.

Lucky Learner Driver

Ntethelelo means forgiveness, but who could FORGIVE that instructor for letting Nonhlanhla pass her driving lesson when she failed to stop in front of red lights. RED LIGHTS. Really? Of course some nosey witnesses said it had something to do with the smart brushing of his leg when she was changing to second gear. Nonhlanhla means luck. Does it get any luckier than that?

The Early Rains

The victims are plagued by a series of nightmares
    and unanswered questions and long-suffering hearts
that can and will turn into something combustible
if their patience continues to wear thin
in shallow graves of denialism and deceit
as if nothing ever happened
the issue of the early rain which washes away the chaff
before the spring rains cannot be wished away or forgotten—
who exactly was behind the grisly massacres and disappearances?
did that early rain seek to wipe out a given group of people
with their languages and cultures and nationhood
or the perceived or real dissidents and supporters?

If I had A Way...

If I had a different passport
    would I brook and nurse
all these painful injuries
and indignities and infirmities
associated with endless bungling
and bullying and butchering?
If I had a way I would have
auctioned it off or had it really
shut down—renovated, rebranded,
revived and released to the communities
of emerging and truly united and civilised nations.
Can I please file divorce papers if its nationhood
would continue to relegate others as second class?
If it could rewind the hand of time
would it make the same old decisions
or do the same old actions it did when
the euphoria of freedom and power was
upon it or would it move with caution
and maturity and treat each and every
citizen with the dignity they deserve?
If I had a way I would choose my own
neighbours and would not live with people
who delight in choosing and tolerating bunglers—
just because they are beneficiaries or tribal loyalists—
but that is as far as it goes since I cannot choose
neighbours and neither can I have my own chosen
leader in a high office or be left alone in an island.
Can`t I disown some people and live in my island?
If this nation were one, our prosperity or suffering
would be one, or would make us one—but clearly
there is a huge gap between those who always have
or enjoy opportunities in terms of jobs and education

and business and politics and rights and everything else
ahead of other citizens. Can`t suffering unite people
and make them see their follies and friends and fiends?
If I had a way weapons of destruction would not be
in careless hands and peace would not be in pieces
because prejudice would be replaced by justice,
corruption would give way to responsibility,
bungling would be swiftly booted out
...and who would not want to live
in a prospering, peaceful
and orderly society?

The Elephantine Call

For their tusks,
    in the name of ivory trade
they are hunted and poached.
Driven to the edge of extinction,
they need complete protection.
Ivory trade ban is the solution.

Africa's Capital

I thought they call you
    Mosi-oa-Tunya ... right?
the world's largest sheet
of fabulously falling water
I thought they call you
mighty Victoria Falls
my dear one of the Seven
Wonders of the World
You set me on safari
to smell and feel and see
the beauty and wonder
of nature in its glory
I see myself bungee-jumping
and white water-rafting
and roaring with the lions
and dancing with the elephants
my dear amazing waterfall
I hear you are also known
as the Adventure
Capital of Africa!

Bring Back Our History And Heritage

You have muddied the waters of
    Our glorious history and heritage
Where shall we hide our long tails?
Our nakedness is now a public feast

The Leopard Man's Fate

The man riding an abused leopard
    feared that if ever he fell down
the animal would chew him up
so he clung on and on to it
he was weary and desperate
he knew the leopard was tired
it ate deprivation and beatings
he feared being disinherited
but the moment of truth
was always approaching
and reproaching him
to repent and leave
the poor animal alone
he okayed himself
he clung on and on
until sleepiness
and tiredness
teamed up
to a thud!

Dance No More

That diminutive spear
    he carries everywhere
is smarter than fear
it abhors hate-mongering
and intolerance of others
different or differing
Ndlovu`s spear spits out
fountains of compassion
and bravely bemoans
the innocents` denigration

One Too Many Losses

What has come over them?
    they have disregarded
the sanctity of life
you say maybe by virtue
of misjudgment?
what has blinded them?
they have authored an orgy
of uncertainties and murders
who are they are policing
by planting seeds of mistrust?

            · · · ·

ARE THESE UMPTEEN MISCARRIAGES
    of justice blind to the fact
    that prejudice breeds
    nothing else
    but jaundice?

Malleable Prospect

Let us reminisce
    and romance
let us rekindle
those fires
of yesteryear
of heart and heat
let us boldly board
a recollection bus
of positive events
of past actions
let us live 'n love
in the present
no matter
how different
because it is all
we can correct
and curve
into our future

The Outlawed Stalker

A voice hounded her ears
    like a stubborn ghost
its cozy compulsion
and invisible invasion
her bitter addiction
in her long dreams
it had a leading role
in her consciousness
it sang her an anthem
it was her sole shadow
its presence forbidden
its intentions unhidden
held her like its only part
like a hapless hostage
her heart ripped apart

Tender-hearted Congratulations

Beloved blessing, as my heart dances and ululates
in honor and celebration of your birthday
I am reminded of how special you are.
Queen of my heart, how can I thank you enough
for your disarming kindness
and understanding?
We might agree to disagree on this and that issue
but by virtue of your commitment and patience
I have learned to unlearn some habits.
We are both learning to be better partners
day in day out thanks to your personality
and the beauty of your heart.
I, for one, would like to proudly and loudly
profess that you have positively changed me
in ways you cannot measure.
I thank you for the warmth in your personality,
for the undying love in your heart
and for being my life partner.

Why The Mforos Were Ditched

Mforo had a damaging disorder
    that did not only see him rout out
and ruin everything in the dance hall
but made life a hell for every sane dancer
and spectator who was not part and parcel
of his plunder- and -slander dance routines.
His better half was no better dancer either
because she suffered from grave rounds
of nasty narcissistic personality disorder
as she swung from one corner to another—
heaping fattened praises and praises upon
her physique and dress code and her hubby.
Some men and women took to the dancefloor
even though the couple trampled upon them
with shameless abandon ...and they danced till
the diplomats and defenders of Mforo safely
defected to the voices and feet of hope and love
and vowed never to look back or to back the Mforos.

The Man's Manifestations

He was not on a cruise ship
    stocked with piles and piles
of clothing and food to sustain
his family for a year or two
Mr. Dewa walked down the road
lost in his world of imagination

• • • •

OBLIVIOUS TO THE HEAVY after- four
    o'clock traffic he murmured

• • • •

AND SOMETIMES STAGGERED in his
    monologue of prayers and fears
    he neither saw nor heard
    his friend and his greeting
    lost and buried in the face
    of an unexampled catastrophe
    that was ringing its bell
    and ushering in a revelation
    his ears and eyes wide-open
    he could not hear or see
    the winding line of cars
    and their occasional farts
    he wondered how man
    had made another person's
    life vulnerable and fearful
    and confused and crazy
    by virtue of greed and power
    and the love of money
    there he was struggling
    with rent and bus fares

yet others could afford
to plan for a calamity

Performer And Giver

They sang and shouted with joy
    as he paced about, whispering of godliness
Suddenly he raised his voice
and approached a young lady
Whose red-painted lips gleamed
with loveliness and chubbiness
He then declared: I see you demon
Leave her lips, I will suck you out!
His 'holy' ones landed on her red ones
He groaned as the congregants shouted 'amen'
Holy Saints! Maybe that demon was stubborn
For their mouths merged madly till sunset!

          . . . .

BREATHLESSLY HE DECLARED victory but added: See me later
    to free you of the last slimy remnants of that monster!
    How could he not be pleased with his powers?
    He who helped the 'heavy-laden' and 'barren' conceive!
    After the labial drama, the pleased Prophet
    ordered his sheep to venture into greener pastures
    There the congregants tucked into dishes of snakes—
    including a menu of stones and flowers and grass
    They washed down the above with purple petrol
    The pleased pastor flashed a batch of flashy cards
    "Tickets to Heaven, economy five hundred dollars
    First class... just eight hundred dollars"

          . . . .

THEY SNAPPED THEM UP, and screamed for more,
    Then the Prophet had a vision: an extra lot coming.
    So he paced about, spraying them with a cute chemical—
    An insect repellant, maybe a perfume?

The dizzy, desperate crowd couldn't have cared less.
What effects would all that drinking and eating have?
Faithfully and obediently they swallowed his poison.
Swiftly dropping to the floor, praising him with their last breath.

Gogo Mahlangu`s Tears And Tales

"It was a terrible time when we were in bondage. Then were had to grapple with the challenges of the war of liberation. We were an expectant and confidant lot". Or so Gogo Mahlangu explains to no one in particular in front of her small mud round hut one Monday evening. Her little walking stick is lying next to her on her reed mat. Gogo is SiNdebele for grandma. She is 102 years old and still going strong . Her memory has not failed her either . For example, she recalls the first words uttered by her first suitor. "I`ve been stalking you for the past six months but I didn`t have the courage to tell you. Today, I want to tell you that you made a fire in my heart that burns forever and ever". There is happiness in her face when she talks about how suitors bought handkerchiefs for the ladies they sought to impress and how the same women pulled off leaves of trees one by one as if uninterested. Her wrinkled face blushes when she talks of the fastness and dishonesty of today`s life. When she harps on her post-independence life rivers of tears punctuate her old cheeks.

Of Scary Second-hand Affairs

Used nappies are courting
    the poor street buyers whilst
second-hand undergarments
are happy to hug their legs
to the poor the lure is too big
they see some street bargains
the concerned citizens bemoan
the dumping of cheap imports
health looks from a distance
with distaste for those who
have brought such misery
and lowness to the citizens
on the pavements some say
they catch sight of second-hand
handkerchiefs and tooth-brushes
proposing love to the poor as well
one male vendor choruses, 'please men—you
know your wives' sizes so buy these old but trendy
panties and bras and petticoats and socks and leggings
for blessed are those under a pretty petticoat government!'

Pauperised

Was it really independence?
or corruption`s pestilence?
Misery was brought. Was
it somehow sold? If it indeed
it was sold ,who in their sane
mind could have bought it?
Is there an auction centre
that can accept it? Is there
a scrapyard that can keep it?
Is there a plausible justification
for that appalling level of stooping
and descent in a community of decent
nations? Is there any nightmare worse?
What was gallant blood shed for? Is that
the same rich land where there was abundant
milk and honey? Or is this a mere plasticised
and pauperised clone pretending to be our
motherland? How long, the basket case?

. . . .

IT WAS PLAINLY THRIVING. Now because of
rampant thieving and bungling—it is
declining and crying infinitely . It is
painfully rapped because of the wolves` rape
of the people` resources and rights?
Really, with that rich and diverse
resource base ,should it not be the pride,
the jewel and the juice of the entire continent?
One day the whining will be over. The shining will
take over. Only when sanity rules supreme over impunity.
And only when justice prevails over prejudice.

The Wrecker's Heart

Does she have a soul?
      does she have a heart?
the poor feast on hunger
the electricity has eloped
people's peace has paled
their presences speckled
her heart is a rough rock
it is a hell of necromancy
one would expect her
to break down in tears
one would expect her
to rue and cry in despair
but that is not the case
with the wrecker of life

Blown Away

The morning sun`s smile was visible
    she wanted to mind her business
walking down the streets of Joburg
the gospel singer`s baritone seemed
to bar her from proceeding with her urgent journey
it was clear that the singer had chosen the repertoire
that suited his instruments and dance routines well
what a musical presence the soloist had—it could
capture passers-by and blow them away to heaven
it was a call from her supervisor –asking her whether
that day she was not going to report for duty—that
brought her to mother earth and had her heart skidding
she weaved and rushed through the ballooning crowd
and upon arriving at her workplace she discovered that
not only was her job on the line but also her little money
was nowhere to be seen or felt in her beautiful handbag

Subzero Fireplace

When has the fireplace
 become the bedroom?
What's the matter here?
Why is the cat sleeping
at the fireplace? Freezing!
What's happening?
Why has fireplace become
blind to breakfast and lunch
and dinner times?
Poverty-stricken pots
agitating for a new cook
who cares and is humanly.

Pre-paid Water Meter

Others strongly believe you are spoiling for a showdown,
Many warn: you are in for a real rude awakening.
Maybe you should just slow down, gauge the mood and retreat.
This fat fact is not to water down your zeal and zest.
Please Pre-paid Water Meter, if you going to make the poor people thirsty,
Do not set foot in our city in spite of our perennial water woes.
We condemn and reject your subtle coming with the mightiest force you deserve,
Pre-paid Water Meter, remember the poor have a basic right to drink safe to water.
Pre-paid Water Meter, do not tell the poor residents about the need to cut down
Operational costs because what they need is clean and affordable water.
What if people would not be able to access clean water because they are failing to buy
The water on a pre-paid basis, should they be condemned to thirst or untreated water?

Carnages Haunting The Present

"People are being hounded like animals for slaughter. Bigotry has taken roots in all our spheres of life because it is now an institutionalised and normalised cancer. It is set to dine with the perpetrators one day if not carefully addressed". One human rightist bemoaned. Someone is saying, "The honesty of that speech of yesteryear makes it a relevant prophecy of today".

The Lake Of Vice And Valour

The traveller marveled at those swimming at the lake of human rights
    they swam against all the odds—their gallantry too awesome to fathom
    the bottomless lake was choking with corrosive dirt and inhuman odour
    the shocked visitor caught sight of kidnapping snakes and sharks of ruin
    he wondered about the whereabouts of the big fish of justice and peace
    and whose overall responsibility was it to ensure the safety of the divers?

The Speaker's Plea

I thought she was a psychologist
    Maybe just an assertive sociologist
But she said she was a geologist
She was telling people that she had a habit
Of digging into people's minds to find out exactly
What type of thought-processes they undertook daily
I listened to her talk about the power of imagination
How it could be an amazing human inspiration
And an incubator and sustainer of civilisation
She declared that there is a difference between imagination
And critical thinking though the two elements are related
And challenged her audience to be critical thinkers

Mopani Worms

Dried and salted
    a delicacy that saw an eater
swallow up his tongue!

Beloved Sitshwala

Mouth-watering stiff dumpling from maize
    gracing today's hot pot

The Birthday Dancer Who Stole The Show

White City Stadium roared into life
As soon as the city's music icon—
Mhleli Mhlophe –also known as
Mhle Magic - took to the stage.
Mhleli's performance was magic
Like his name. He had his audience
Eating out of his hand. His many fans
Filled the council-run stadium to capacity.
Mhle Magic's birthday was a big bash.
Meat was plentiful. Ten fat cattle had
Been butchered .Drinks of all sorts flew
down the throats of the attendees in style.
When the big party was over, tongues
Started wagging. Unpopular politicians
Called him a little regionalist. Some even
Went to the extent of labeling him a copycat.
Nothing had been stranger than the antics of
A drunk dancer who had the party-goers
Blushing. She had everyone gasping in shock
When her figure gyrated live in its naked glory.

Tennis Star On The Horizon

I think she is set to break records.
    Her heart has been broken several times by the cynical and silly decrees and labels and ideas of relatives who confine her world to her disability. She has shot out of their little box of confinement and got some tongues wagging. How could she ever dream of playing tennis with such weak arms? How could she dream big, wax great? She has refused to wallow in self-pity. Playing tennis and netball -she has endeared herself to her teachers and her classmates. A class monitor, she commands respect on the court.

The Tussle Between Patience And Polite

Polite hammered impolite knocks on the door,
    Patience detonated some impatient snoring sounds.
"Hey you, Patience, I know you are in there. Open up
the door, *maaan*! You're not asleep either!" shouted Polite.
As if Patience wanted to show Polite that patience
is indeed a virtue, she continued feigning sleepiness.
Polite was frothing on the mouth, making some impolite remarks
about a silly boyfriend-habouring harlot, when the landlady arrived...

Do You Know Bulawayo?

I overheard something that made me
go back into life, that made my heart
cry and bleed, that made my head spin.
Mothers were asking their children
whether they knew Bulawayo: the
real Bulawayo, the City of Kings.
They were asking them whether they
knew Barbourfields Stadium, the real BF,
also fondly known as Emagumeni.
They told their stunned children that long ago
people loved their national broadcasting
stations, both radio and TV.
They spoke glowingly about some radio
and TV personalities and programmes that
kept them glued to their speakers or screens.
They were asking them whether they had
heard of such crowd-pulling programmes
like "Ngisakhumbula" or "Ezemuli"?
They were saying recreational centres
had gone into extinction in Bulawayo.
Where is the Gwabalanda Tennis Court?
They bemoaned the disappearance of
the real G & D Shoes (PVT) Lt, and the
real Dairibord and National Railways.
They lamented the loss of lustre
the International Trade Fair in Bulawayo was
associated with. All they saw was a dumb squid.
"Butcheries were not known to sell chicken heads.
We were not known to rely on bones for relish like dogs.
Neither did we depend on veggies like rabbits," they declared.
They claimed that some Mickey Mouse business
had eclipsed Bulawayo`s development agenda -

citing the influx of hijackers and mercenaries.
Do you know Bulawayo? they asked.
Not Hillbrow, not Sunnyside, not Soweto either.
Bulawayo in its true colours and metropolitan beauty?
They were playing the 80's & 90's music,
admiring citizens who lived and thrived
in a magnificent and stimulating city.
They were playing Lovemore Majaivana
of Ngifuna Imali fame, they were playing
the Dalom Kids and the Soul Brothers too.
They were begging providence to turn back
the hand of time, they were not dancing but
pinching their bodies for sobriety and approval.
They were asking their children whether they knew
some of their relatives in foreign, distant lands;
those who disappeared and never returned.
They were asking their children whether they
knew beauty: real life, true freedom to live life
at home in an abundant and dignified fashion.
They were asking their teens whether they knew
money: local currency, the 50 cent coin that
could buy them a bottle of soft drink; yes, 50c!
They were asking them whether they knew
that at Mafakela Primary school and other
institutions, kids used to be served free milk.
They were asking their youngsters whether they
had ever felt the aroma that used to emanate
from a certain Bulawayo confectionery.
Did they know that it was once taboo in Bulawayo
to see residents being settled in a new suburb
without crucial amenities like functioning toilets?
They said it was unheard of in Bulawayo to see officials
hand over suburbs which did not have running water
or whose roads were in a deplorable state.
They were telling them that the moment

one saw the words "Welcome to Bulawayo",
the city's appeal greeted one warmly.
It was a refreshing sight: the smiling lights,
the vibrating factories, the well-maintained
buildings and roads, a true majestic presence.
Not a disheartening signature: the frowning sight
of darkness, the deathly silence of the industrial
site and the potholed roads and distraught dwellers.
They were talking about Bulawayo's cleanliness,
the joviality and hospitality of an organised people
who loved and celebrated life and treasured humanity.
Not a deformity, a scrap yard: the ghost and the ruins
their children call a city, not the nightmare the residents
grapple with, not the decay and damage they agonise over.
Then as I drifted away from them, I saw and heard
the determination in the faces and voices of both mothers
and their offspring to make Bulawayo live and shine again.

The Past Catching Up With Him

For money they said he lost his soul
    And found nothing, nothing foul
About the gangs` depravity
He basked in their immorality
Till they turned him into irrelevancy
A brand new team sought transparency
They accused him of feasting with stray dogs
And said: deal with the fleas and our legal logs

A Simple Sweet Snuggle

A shy sweet stroke
    on a searching shoulder
revealed a sensitivity
to how sensations
can carry a real riot

Of Fussing, Fasting And Fastening

Zero but dosh was being chased
    petite was a poor civilian`s waist
in a rich plot broken and broke
while vanity in high office spoke
of the need to tighten our tiny waists
and have no desire for social tastes
as heaven was on its way, not in haste
it did not mention the worst of waste
that exhibited itself through neglect—
talk of luxury hires and all for the select
they feasted, and got fat purses & bodies
a legacy of profligacy, that`s what it embodies
while the ordinary citizens fasted & fainted
one man proposed that such men be sainted
someone yelled of being screwed by a vulture!
the toady said: let's sacrifice for a better future!

Their Beautiful Bae

Glad tidings he brought to his family
that he had found a soulmate, a lovely
princess and all that jazz which precision
of language cannot pinpoint, his decision
to ditch bachelorship was received well,
the unmarried state of me, I say farewell,
he declared till it became naked that he
and his deadly dad dated the same bae!

Global Social Conscience

It was zoomed on Zoom
   A talk on social conscience
On shared values and duties
On diversity and dignity
On empathy and solidarity
The speakers consented
To a co-existence of plants
And animals on this globe
They said this is obligatory
Those who fail on that score
Can look for other spheres
For both flora and faunas
Are knottily interdependent
Humans come in several sizes
Thus the need to experience
A sense of love and belonging
To a shared or common humanity
Is an issue that cannot be overstated

Stormy Seas And Heartbreaks

Sinking in poverty every day
    They sought a life worth living
A boat planned to carry them
To a land of fortune collapsed
In the Mediterranean as lives
And dreams were shattered

Dear 2020, What's My Quote Of The Year?

A year that has socially alienated us, a year
that has mobilised & demobilised us through
quarantines, a year that has not only confused
the entire humanity but has also confined it
We have learned lessons on physical, social,
emotional, mental impacts of the virus, about
resilience & self-love, about being productive
and positive ,about precautions & protocols
We have lost loved ones, professions, prospects;
but recovered the ultimate love, a love for life,
a love for humanity, a love for a better world,
we have revived the need to mop up the virus

. . . .

A YEAR THAT HAS BEEN financially challenging
for individuals, institutions, families & nations,
A year that has reminded us of the significance
of keeping safe, healthy, in touch & hoping
A year that seen my writing career pick up,
A year in which teachers learned to teach
outside the box while students & parents
turned their homes into virtual classrooms

. . . .

A YEAR CHARACTERISED by a series of arguments
& counterarguments, controversies & theories;
In areas of high exposure, queries on whether
to mask up , have a lockdown or not, shot up
A year that has been more riotous than
any of us could have fathomed or imagined,
Dear 2020 when I said, "can this get worse?"
it was a rhetorical question, not a contest!

Dear 2020, guess what my quote of the year is? It`s not "2020 you have been unlike any other we have experienced". It`s "thou shalt not covid thy neighbor`s life, wear a mask" by Arianna!

Biography

••••

SIBANDA IS THE AUTHOR of *Notes, Themes, Things And Other Things, The Gushungo Way, Sleeping Rivers, Love O'clock, The Dead Must Be Sobbing, Football of Fools, Cutting-edge Cache: Unsympathetic Untruth, Of the Saliva and the Tongue, When Inspiration Sings In Silence, The Way Forward, This Cannot be Happening: Speaking truth To Power, The Ndaba Jamela* Collections, *Poetry Pharmacy, Sometimes Seasons Come With Unseasonal Harvests, As If They Minded: The Loudness Of Whispers, The Dangers Of Child Marriages: Billions Of Dollars Lost In Earnings And Human Capital* and *The Art Of Making An Artwork: As Dramatic And Enigmatic As We Know It To Be* and *Timebomb: Before The Spring Rains.* . Ndaba was nominated for the following awards: *National Arts Merit Awards, Mary Ballard Poetry Chapbook Prize, The Pushcart Prize* and *Best of the Net*.

Sibanda's book *Notes, Themes, Things And Other Things: Confronting Controversies ,Contradictions And Indoctrinations* was considered for The **2019 Restless Book Prize for New Immigrant Writing in Nonfiction.** Ndaba's other forthcoming book *Cabinet Meetings: Of Big And Small Preys* was considered for *The Graywolf Press Africa Prize 2018*.

Some of Sibanda's works are found or forthcoming in *Page & Spine, Peeking Cat, Piker Press , SCARLET LEAF REVIEW , Universidad Complutense de Madrid, the Pangolin Review, Kalahari Review ,Botsotso, The Ofi Press Magazine, Hawaii Pacific Review, Deltona How, The song is*[1], *Indian Review*[2], *Eunoia Review*[3], *JONAH magazine*[4], *Saraba Magazine*[5], *Poetry Potion*[6], *Saraba*

---

1. http://www.google.com.kw/
url?sa=t&rct=j&q=&esrc=s&source=web&cd=31&cad=rja&uact=8&ved=0ahUKEwixxIfq1L7aAhVMEV AKHWyzBr04HhAWCCQwAA&url=http%3A%2F%2Fthesongis.blogspot.com%2F2016%2F10%2Fwelcome-to-ndaba-sibanda.html&usg=AOvVaw3ywRpJEmWVpdeo9oRc0G6k

2. http://www.google.com.kw/
url?sa=t&rct=j&q=&esrc=s&source=web&cd=34&cad=rja&uact=8&ved=0ahUKEwixxIfq1L7aAhVMEV AKHWyzBr04HhAWCDQwAw&url=http%3A%2F%2Findianreview.in%2Fauthor%2Fndaba-sibanda%2F&usg=AOvVaw0yqoWxQanXdNI57DborUHc

3. https://www.google.com.kw/ url?sa=t&rct=j&q=&esrc=s&source=web&cd=36&cad=rja&uact=8&ved=0ahUKEwixxIfq1L7aAhVMEVAKHWyzBr04HhAWCD8wBQ&url=https%3A%2F%2Feunoiareview.wordpress.com%2Ftag%2Fndaba-sibanda%2F&usg=AOvVaw3cDwM55nSjywT4KizEVm1Z

4. https://www.google.com.kw/ url?sa=t&rct=j&q=&esrc=s&source=web&cd=38&cad=rja&uact=8&ved=0ahUKEwixxIfq1L7aAhVMEVAKHWyzBr04HhAWCEkwBw&url=https%3A%2F%2Fjonahmagazine.com%2Fcategory%2Fndaba-sibanda%2F&usg=AOvVaw1XuDmiqnQXv0mn6ah21vRL

5. https://www.google.com.kw/ url?sa=t&rct=j&q=&esrc=s&source=web&cd=12&cad=rja&uact=8&ved=0ahUKEwjd39fE0b7aAhURalAKHW8aDA84ChAWCCowAQ&url=https%3A%2F%2Fsarabamag.com%2Fauthor%2Fndaba-sibanda%2F&usg=AOvVaw2E7FVhMW8qqz0n3viFAa8l

6. http://www.google.com.kw/ url?sa=t&rct=j&q=&esrc=s&source=web&cd=16&cad=rja&uact=8&ved=0ahUKEwjd39fE0b7aAhURalAKHW8aDA84ChAWCDwwBQ&url=http%3A%2F%2Fwww.poetrypotion.com%2Fbhalagwe-by-ndaba-sibanda%2F&usg=AOvVaw0nHhEou4Nu0Ma7Hdo0rBvD

Magazine[7], Poetry Potion[8], The Borfski Press[9], Snippets[10], East Coast Literary Review[11], Random Poem Tree[12], festival-of-language and Whispering Prairie Press[13]

Ndaba blogs here: *Let's Get Cracking! – Ndaba Sibanda - WordPress.com*[14]

---

7. https://www.google.com.kw/
url?sa=t&rct=j&q=&esrc=s&source=web&cd=12&cad=rja&uact=8&ved=0ahUKEwjd39fE0b7aAhURalAKHW8aDA84ChAWCCowAQ&url=https%3A%2F%2Fsarabamag.com%2Fauthor%2Fndaba-sibanda%2F&usg=AOvVaw2E7FVhMW8qqz0n3viFAa8l

8. http://www.google.com.kw/
url?sa=t&rct=j&q=&esrc=s&source=web&cd=16&cad=rja&uact=8&ved=0ahUKEwjd39fE0b7aAhURalAKHW8aDA84ChAWCDwvBQ&url=http%3A%2F%2Fwww.poetrypotion.com%2Fbhalagwe-by-ndaba-sibanda%2F&usg=AOvVaw0nHhEou4Nu0Ma7Hdo0rBvD

9. https://www.google.com.kw/
search?sa=N&biw=1188&bih=541&tbm=bks&q=inauthor:%22The+Borfski+Press%22&ved=0ahUKEwix1ve51r7aAhVHKlAKHb9uAbU4KBD0CAhNMAg

10. https://books.google.co.zw/
books?id=u0gDBAAAQBAJ&pg=PP6&lpg=PP6&dq=ndaba+sibanda&source=bl&ots=F-dFSyex0h&sig=OU8S-8EsUDultt_CwtXjTG0WsuM&hl=en&sa=X&ved=0ahUKEwj94eji177aAhWIalAKHezADBw4MhDoAQgkMAA

11. http://www.google.com.kw/
url?sa=t&rct=j&q=&esrc=s&source=web&cd=59&cad=rja&uact=8&ved=0ahUKEwj94eji177aAhWIalAKHezADBw4MhAWCE4wCA&url=http%3A%2F%2Fwww.eastcoastliteraryreview.com%2Ffeatured-writers.html&usg=AOvVaw3ch6EKIpttipYfTvqD1xvR

12. https://www.google.com.kw/
url?sa=t&rct=j&q=&esrc=s&source=web&cd=65&cad=rja&uact=8&ved=0ahUKEwiynofn2b7aAhXFKVAKHUh-Cw44PBAWCDkwBA&url=https%3A%2F%2Frandompoemtree.wordpress.com%2F2018%2F03%2F08%2Fthe-time-is-here-by-ndaba-sibanda%2F&usg=AOvVaw1W1mz8QVBARPwjUgW9jJaK

13. http://www.google.com.kw/
url?sa=t&rct=j&q=&esrc=s&source=web&cd=11&cad=rja&uact=8&ved=0ahUKEwif6ZTU3b7aAhUHZ1AKHUTFCcM4ChAWCCQwAA&url=http%3A%2F%2Fwww.wppress.org%2Fmain%2Fwp-content%2Fuploads%2F2014%2F11%2Fvol_12_preview.pdf&usg=AOvVaw3b7HidRu6cAveVnbP_O23K

14. https://www.google.com.kw/
url?sa=t&rct=j&q=&esrc=s&source=web&cd=46&cad=rja&uact=8&ved=0ahUKEwix1ve51r7aAh

VHKlAKHb9uAbU4KBAWCDwwBQ&url=https%3A%2F%2Fndabasibanda.wordpress.com%2F201 7%2F03%2F26%2Ffirst-blog-post%2F&usg=AOvVaw1yYq1FDDJ38IdZJ777Ocsp

www.ingramcontent.com/pod-product-compliance
Lightning Source LLC
LaVergne TN
LVHW051519070426
835507LV00023B/3204